Back Porch
BLESSINGS

Back Porch
BLESSINGS

A COLLECTION OF MY WRITINGS
AND YOUR THOUGHTS

Staci Holland Pealock

CROSSBOOKS
PUBLISHING

CrossBooks™
A Division of LifeWay
1663 Liberty Drive
Bloomington, IN 47403
www.crossbooks.com
Phone: 1-866-879-0502

First published by CrossBooks 12/1/2010

ISBN: 978-1-6150-7667-3 (sc)
ISBN: 978-1-6150-7668-0 (dj)

Library of Congress Control Number: 2010941458

Printed in the United States of America

Scripture quotations marked NLT are taken from the Holy Bible, New Living Translation, copyright 1996, 2004. Used by permission of Tyndale House Publishers, Inc., Wheaton, Illinois 60189. All rights reserved.

Scripture taken from the HOLY BIBLE, NEW INTERNATIONAL VERSION®. Copyright © 1973, 1978, 1984 Biblica. Used by permission of Zondervan. All rights reserved.

Scripture quotations taken from the New American Standard Bible®, Copyright © 1960, 1962, 1963, 1968, 1971, 1972, 1973, 1975, 1977, 1995 by The Lockman Foundation. Used by permission." (www.Lockman.org)

Scripture quotations taken from the King James Version of the Holy Bible.

Scripture taken from the New King James Version. Copyright 1979, 1980, 1982 by Thomas Nelson, inc. Used by permission. All rights reserved.

Scriptures marked as "(CEV)" are taken from the Contemporary English Version Copyright © 1995 by American Bible Society. Used by permission.

This book is printed on acid-free paper.

Any people depicted in stock imagery provided by Thinkstock are models, and such images are being used for illustrative purposes only. Certain stock imagery © Thinkstock.

Dedication

This book is dedicated to my sweet Nanny Lois. She has always been an inspiration to me. She is my biggest fan. When I write anything, she is the first to hear it. And she always responds the same way: "Oh, Staci, that is so beautiful, make sure you write that down and send me a copy." So, Nanny, here is your copy of my *Back Porch Blessings*!

Also, I thank my precious husband, Todd, and our two blessings from above, Ansley and Andrew. You are the joys of my life. Thanks for all your encouragement. It means everything to me!

I Love You, Child!

I love you, child, no need to dread

I love you, child, I know what's ahead

I love you, child, I'll see you through

I love you, child, I know what to do

I love you, child, stay close to me

I love you, child, just believe.

I'm on your side and fighting for,
you're the one I love and adore.

No earthly mind could ever see,
what I have in store when you believe.

Trust in me and all my ways,
I'll give you life throughout your days.

I love you, child, oh yes I do,
I love you, child, do you love you?

Isaiah 30:18 (New Living Translation)

So the LORD must wait for you to come to Him so he can
show you his love and compassion. For the LORD is a faithful
God. Blessed are those who wait for His help.

*Do you know that you are loved by God? In what special ways has He shown
you lately that He loves you?*

_____

_____

_____

_____

_____

_____

_____

_____

_____

_____

_____

_____

_____

_____

_____

_____

_____

_____

Thank You, Lord, for Your unconditional love!

Save the Date

All the hurt and rocky places,
every time you looked to wrong faces
I was here, patient to wait,
for I knew our Destiny Date.

Do you not see what I can do,
if only to me you live right and true.
I am here, patient I wait;
will you attend our Destiny Date?

Take that first step onto the water, get out of that boat.
I promise, you will not sink, but surely you will float.
We have a date with destiny, my dear,
your invitation is right here.

You need not fret or worry at all,
just know I'll answer when you call.
We have a date with destiny, my dear,
run to me and do not fear.

Walk in Faith, and believe me to do
all the wonderful things I have shown you.
We have a date with destiny, my dear,
I am waiting, please meet me here.
My arms are open wide;
please let me walk by your side.

Oh, yes, we have a date with destiny, my dear!

Ecclesiastes 6:10 (New Living Translation)

Everything has already been decided. It was known long ago
what each person would be. So there's no use arguing with
God about your destiny.

Have you had your date with destiny? What are you waiting on? Share your
heart with the Lord; let Him know you are ready for your date with destiny,
my dear.

_____

_____

_____

_____

_____

_____

_____

_____

_____

_____

_____

_____

_____

_____

_____

Thank You, Lord, for my destiny!

Brokenness to Beauty

In my brokenness, the Lord sees my beauty.
In my weakness, He finds my strength.

When tears flow like a river
through my broken heart,
The Lord applies His ointment
and gives me courage to
make a fresh start.

Only He knows the depth of my love,
but to express with words just isn't enough.

So with my life, I daily will show,
the God in heaven I want everyone to know.

Psalm 34:18 (New International Version)

The LORD is close to the brokenhearted
and saves those who are crushed in spirit.

Have you experienced brokenness? How did God take it and make it beautiful for His glory?

_____

_____

_____

_____

_____

_____

_____

_____

_____

_____

_____

_____

_____

_____

_____

_____

Thank You, Lord, for making me beautiful!

Thank You, Daddy!

It's so sweet how the Holy Spirit sweeps over me
and makes everything right again in my life.

Tears streaming down my face,
my stomach yearning to be filled with all I can stand.

My heart is heavy
and beating for the will of God in my life.

With every breath I can smell
the sweet savor of God surrounding me.

I wish I could grab God and hug him and never let go,
and melt in his compassionate arms.

Be his little girl, looking up to her Daddy!

Mark 5:34 (New Living Translation)

And He said to her, "Daughter, your faith has made you well.
Go in peace. Your suffering is over."

Are you a Daddy's girl? Well, you can start today. Climb up into your Daddy's lap and tell him what's on your mind. He enjoys your company.

_____

_____

_____

_____

_____

_____

_____

_____

_____

_____

_____

_____

_____

_____

_____

_____

_____

Thank You, Lord, that I'm a Daddy's girl!

In Memory of "Maw" Tater

She didn't have a lot to give away,
But she shared her love each and every day

Love, Laughter, Smile, and Donkey Call,
Just a few memories of a lady we called Maw.

She had two daughters and two sons on Earth,
Three sons in heaven awaiting her.

Wish more people could have Maw Taylor's ways,
Made this home a better place to stay.

Her big heart for lovin' and sweet arms for huggin',
Eyes that were dancin' and feet that were prancin'.

Now she dwells on Heaven's Shore,
If only I see our Maw once more.

I can envision her right now,
leaping and rejoicing, wearing a heavenly crown.

She has a radiant smile on her face,
as she sings to GOD, "Amazing Grace."

One of Maw's heart's desires,
That no one would perish in hell's fire.

Listen to me, my friend,
Maw wants to see you again.
Make peace with JESUS and you shall abide,
On Heaven's Sweet Shore with Maw by your side.

We love and miss you, Maw

Psalm 116:15 (King James Version)

Precious in the sight of the LORD is the death of His saints.

Death is not the ending for our loved ones, because they're just truly beginning to live. Share a special memory of someone who has gone to be with Jesus.

_____

_____

_____

_____

_____

_____

_____

_____

_____

_____

_____

_____

_____

_____

_____

_____

_____

_____

Thank You, Lord, for comfort!

Look at Your Scars ...

Scars don't have to be a reminder of the hurt, but of the healing. While it may have appeared that I had a lot of negatives in my life, my childhood was sweet and simple. The bumps in the road only made me realize that sometimes life is like that. You work really hard, and you still can hit a bump. Everything in your cart falls out—not lost, just spilled. As you gather it together again, you learn that it's the end; just a little more work is required of you.

If I could go back and change my life, I would not because the bumps made me who I am today. And I think I'm doing just fine. My dreams and prayers are coming through. And we all know the best teachers are the ones who have first been taught the lesson.

So, that's why I say scars do not have to remind us of the hurt but of the healing in Jesus's name.

Isaiah 53:5 (King James Version)

But he was wounded for our transgressions, he was bruised for
our iniquities: the chastisement of our peace was upon him;
and with his stripes we are healed.

*Look at the scar(s) on your heart. What do you see, hurt or healing? Write a
prayer below, and ask the Lord to heal your wounds. He took the beating so
you don't have to.*

_____

_____

_____

_____

_____

_____

_____

_____

_____

_____

_____

_____

_____

Thank You, Lord, for healing!

Is There a God?

When my son was ten years old, he asked me, "Mama, how do you know there really is a God?" I handed him my Bible and said, "Take this, and ask God to show you that He is real." It wasn't five minutes until Andrew was running back to me. His eyes were wide open, and he was talking so fast. "Mama, Mama, I know God is real—look what He showed me." God led Andrew to open the Bible to Psalm 53. He had underlined the entire chapter in my Bible. To this day, when I see that underlined passage in my Bible, it as if God is reminding me who He is.

Psalm 53:1–6 (New Living Translation)

<u>*¹Only fools say in their hearts, "There is no God." They are corrupt, and their actions are evil; not one of them does good! ²God looks down from heaven on the entire human race; He looks to see if anyone is truly wise, if anyone seeks God. ³But no, all have turned away; all have become corrupt. No one does good, not a single one! ⁴Will those who do evil never learn? They eat up my people like bread and wouldn't think of praying to God. ⁵Terror will grip them, terror like they have never known before. God will scatter the bones of your enemies. You will put them to shame, for God has rejected them. ⁶Who will come from* Mount Zion *to rescue* Israel? *When God restores His people, Jacob will shout with joy, and Israel will rejoice*</u>

14

Psalm 53:1

Only fools say in their hearts, "There is no God."

Has God ever spoken to you directly from His Word? Share the circumstances and the passage of Scripture that He gave to you.

_____

_____

_____

_____

_____

_____

_____

_____

_____

_____

_____

_____

_____

_____

_____

_____

_____

Thank You, Lord, for revelation!

Before My Eyes

As the sun begins to rise,
what's that I see before my eyes?

Love and mercy flowing through,
love and mercy from Me to you.

Sometime it seems that all is lost,
that the price is more than the cost.

Walking and learning what to do,
trust in Me to see you through.

Why sometimes I feel all alone,
why sometimes I feel right at home?

Now, My sweet precious Friend,
I can bless you from beginning to end.

So, on this bright and sweet fresh morn,
I run to You and turn away from scorn.

Many faces to shine my love upon,
many races to be won.

No time for anger or for being afraid,
we have work to do; let's get started today!

Psalm 19:8 (New International Version)

The precepts of the LORD are right, giving joy to the heart.
The commands of the LORD are radiant, giving light to the
eyes.

*We have all seen dark days. Share a time when in darkness, the radiant light
of the Lord opened your eyes, bringing you joy and encouragement.*

_____

_____

_____

_____

_____

_____

_____

_____

_____

_____

_____

_____

_____

_____

_____

_____

Thank You, Lord, for opening my eyes!

How Can Hurt Turn into Peace?

When you've been hurt so deeply within,

you find yourself without a friend.

There's no place to run or hide,

you're alone, with no one by your side.

Go to your knees in prayer.

Cry out to God.

For you know He's always near.

Then as sweet as honeysuckle

blowing in the breeze,

God meets with you while on your knees.

Then so softly I hear Him speak:

"Don't worry, my child,

I am here for your needs to meet.

I'll turn your hurt around,

just let go

and peace will be found."

Psalm 85:8 (New Living Translation)

I listen carefully to what God the Lord is saying, for He
speaks peace to his faithful people.
But let them not return to their foolish ways.

*Can you hear me now? What peaceful words are being spoken over your life
today by our sweet Lord?*

_____

_____

_____

_____

_____

_____

_____

_____

_____

_____

_____

_____

_____

_____

_____

_____

Thank You, Lord, for speaking!

Close Your Eyes ...

Now smell the

Freshness of the

Rain after a

Quick summer

Shower!

So is it for our soul,

When our Lord sends His

Refreshment!

Romans 15:32 (New International Version)

So that by God's will I may come to you with joy and together
with you be refreshed.

*Have you ever been dry in your Spirit? And God sent a refreshing rain that
washed away all the dust from your heart. How did you experience this
cleansing?*

_____

_____

_____

_____

_____

_____

_____

_____

_____

_____

_____

_____

_____

_____

_____

_____

Thank You, Lord, for refreshment!

Broken Vessel

God takes the vessel that's been cracked and crumbled by the harshness of the world. He places his gentle, loving touch on the broken piece. He puts the pieces together again and bonds them with His Spirit. And while there may be some evidence of a crack or two, He holds us together.

For God is our
"super glue."

Psalm 34:17–19 (New International Version)

[17]The righteous cry out, and the LORD hears them; he delivers them from all their troubles. [18]The LORD is close to the brokenhearted and saves those who are crushed in spirit. [19]A righteous man may have many troubles, but the LORD delivers him from them all.

It is not God's desire for His vessels to be broken. Do you have an area that is broken? Please allow God access so He can apply His healing ointment.

_____

_____

_____

_____

_____

_____

_____

_____

_____

_____

_____

_____

_____

_____

_____

_____

Thank You, Lord, for healing!

How in Weakness Am I Strong?

When times are tough and dreary,

and oh, my soul is so weary.

And Your name I will call

to find my strength and not fall.

I feel Your arms, so big and strong,

picking me up and carrying me along.

So in my weakness,

You make me strong.

2 Corinthians 12:10(New International Version)

That is why, for Christ's sake, I delight in weaknesses, in
insults, in hardships, in persecutions, in difficulties. For when
I am weak, then I am strong.

*Are you weary from battle? Let God fight for you. Write a prayer, thanking
God for giving you His strength through your weakness.*

_____

_____

_____

_____

_____

_____

_____

_____

_____

_____

_____

_____

_____

_____

_____

_____

Thank You, Lord, for Your Strength!

The Light

Who is the light that shines from above,
sending down His gentle love?

God Himself in perfect peace,
giving my heart sweet release.

Holding nothing back from my Lord,
with Him I let my Spirit soar.

Looking up, I feel God's grace,
until that day I see His face.

Psalm 25:7 (New Living Translation)

Do not remember the rebellious sins of my youth. Remember me in the light of Your unfailing love, for You are merciful, O LORD.

How can you shine the light of God's unfailing love?

_____

_____

_____

_____

_____

_____

_____

_____

_____

_____

_____

_____

_____

_____

_____

_____

Thank You, Lord, for unfailing love!

Eyes of Worry or a Heart of Trust

Do you have eyes that worry over
everything you see?

Or a heart of trust that
simply believes?

Give God all your burdens, big or small,
He can surely handle them all!

Philippians 4:6 (Contemporary English Version)

⁶Don't worry about anything, but pray about everything. With thankful hearts, offer up your prayers and requests to God.

Do you trust God to meet your needs and keep you in His care? If you are struggling with trust, write a prayer and ask the Lord for His wisdom.

_____

_____

_____

_____

_____

_____

_____

_____

_____

_____

_____

_____

_____

_____

_____

_____

_____

_____

Thank You, Lord, for being trustworthy!

Thank You!

Lord, I thank You for Your
MERCY;
it's so undeserved.

Lord, I thank You for Your
WISDOM
sent down from above.

Lord, I thank You for Your
SALVATION
all wrapped up in love.

Lord, I thank You for Your
PEACE
and for giving me enough.

Lord, I thank You for it all
from the beginning to the end,
and mostly
for being my *Friend*!

Proverbs 18:24 (New International Version)

A man of many companions may come to ruin,
but there is a friend who sticks closer than a brother.

Many friendships represent different seasons of our lives. GOD is a friend who is always "in season." How has GOD shown you that He is a true friend who will never let you down?

_____

_____

_____

_____

_____

_____

_____

_____

_____

_____

_____

_____

_____

_____

_____

Thank You, Lord, for being my best friend!

Traveling Shoes

It's been a journey traveling through,
not always easy and not sure what to do.
But time's growing near for
puttin' on my traveling shoes.

Jesus called, and I understood
what He already knew.
It's time for my traveling shoes.

I'm not afraid—no fear, no dread,
looking to Jesus up ahead.
My time here was short, and days were few.
Guess I should be a-lacin' up my traveling shoes.

No pain as I take His hand.
Now I hear Him say, "Let's stand."
Look at me standing anew
and I am wearin' my traveling shoes.

I'm ready to walk on the streets of gold,
the Pearly Gates I'll soon behold.
Jesus told me, "Go on through."
So, I took my first steps in my traveling shoes.

Don't despair, don't be blue.
I'm going to tell you what to do.
Give your heart to Jesus and you will too
be ready for wearin' your traveling shoes.

In loving memory of
Papa John and Uncle Chuckie

Ephesians 6:15 (New Living Translation)

For shoes, put on the peace that comes from the Good News
so that you will be fully prepared.

There is nothing more peaceful than being by the bedside of a loved one who is prepared to come home. I believe it's the angels all around that bring such peace. Share the peace that came during a time of loss. It's only God who can do this for you!

_____

_____

_____

_____

_____

_____

_____

_____

_____

_____

_____

_____

_____

_____

_____

_____

Thank You, Lord, for my traveling shoes!

Tears

Tears of Joy

Tears of Hurt

Tears of Laughter

Tears of Loss

Tears of Love

Tears of Sadness

Tears of Thankfulness

Tears of Fear

Tears of Kindness

Tears of Sickness

Tears of Goodness

Tears of Surrender

Psalm 56:8 (New Living Translation)

You keep track of all my sorrows.
You have collected all my tears in your bottle.
You have recorded each one in your book.

Whatever the reason for your tears, just remember: it is a language God understands. So maybe today you need to speak the language of tears.

_____

_____

_____

_____

_____

_____

_____

_____

_____

_____

_____

_____

_____

_____

Thank You, Lord, for collecting my tears!

We are blessed when we practice ...

Turning the other cheek

Speaking in love

Forgiving false words

Helping one another

Job 36:11 (New Living Translation)

"If they listen and obey God,
they will be blessed with prosperity throughout their lives.
All their years will be pleasant."

You cannot right all the wrongs done to you. What you can do is look to God; He will make it right. "Press through your mess"—that's where you get your "message"!

_____

_____

_____

_____

_____

_____

_____

_____

_____

_____

_____

_____

_____

_____

_____

Thank You, Lord, for my message!

The Bible is the road map to heaven ...

Don't be afraid to ask for direction!

Proverbs 3:5-6 (Contemporary English Version)

⁵With all your heart you must trust the LORD and not your own judgment ⁶Always let Him lead you, and He will clear the road for you to follow.

God always has a plan; do you trust Him to lead you?

_____

_____

_____

_____

_____

_____

_____

_____

_____

_____

_____

_____

_____

_____

_____

_____

_____

_____

Thank You, Lord, for direction!

Divine Design

His body broken in submission,
to His Father's plan

His blood spilled out,
pouring across the land

Crying, "Father, forgive them,
they know not what they do."

A price was paid that day,
for me and you.

You are special,
you are one of a kind

God made you a
DIVINE DESIGN!

Psalm 139:13 (New Living Translation)

You made all the delicate, inner parts of my body
and knit me together in my mother's womb.

You are beautiful. Go look in the mirror right now and say, "I am beautiful!"
God doesn't make mistakes or junk! YOU ARE BEAUTIFUL! Do you feel
like a divine design? I hope so, because you are!

_____

_____

_____

_____

_____

_____

_____

_____

_____

_____

_____

_____

_____

_____

_____

_____

Thank You, Lord, for making me a divine design!

Love?

Do I really understand what love is and isn't?

Does love compensate or condemn?

Does love "do it my way" or say "no way"?

Does love radiate acceptance or rejection?

Does love make us vulnerable or build walls?

Does love have conditions, or is it unconditional?

Does love look through eyes of judgment or

of understanding?

Does love build up or tear down?

You can never underestimate the power of unconditional love. I never believed in unconditional love until recently, during my Bible study. The Lord opened my eyes to something marvelous. Love is powerful! It can cover a multitude of mistakes. It has a purpose and a plan. It says "way to go!" It's an open book. It has no wrong. It is "come as you are," no matter who or what you are. It gives you strength.

You see, the "it" in the story doesn't refer to you or me. It is GOD! So love is what we make it in our lives, and GOD is the source of love. If we have GOD, we have His unconditional love flowing through us for one another. YAY! We can love unconditionally! Love is it! It is GOD!

1 Corinthians 13:4-7 (New Living Translation)

[4]Love is patient and kind. Love is not jealous or boastful or proud [5]or rude. It does not demand its own way. It is not irritable, and it keeps no record of being wronged. [6]It does not rejoice about injustice but rejoices whenever the truth wins out. [7]Love never gives up, never loses faith, is always hopeful, and endures through every circumstance.

Use the space below to rewrite the above scripture replacing your name for the words "love" and "it." WOW! That's powerful! You are loved, and you are LOVE!

_____

_____

_____

_____

_____

_____

_____

_____

_____

_____

_____

_____

_____

Thank You, Lord, for love!

Feed it and it will grow,

Starve it and it will die!

Galatians 6:7–8 (The Message)

Don't be misled: No one makes a fool of God. What a person plants, he will harvest. The person who plants selfishness, ignoring the needs of others—ignoring God!—harvests a crop of weeds. All he'll have to show for his life is weeds! But the one who plants in response to God, letting God's Spirit do the growth work in him, harvests a crop of real life, eternal life.

What are you sowing and growing today?

_____

_____

_____

_____

_____

_____

_____

_____

_____

_____

_____

_____

_____

_____

_____

_____

_____

Thank you, Lord, for the harvest!

It's My Time

Day is dawning into night.
It's my time.

It may seem wrong, but all is right.
It's my time.

My work on Earth is finally done.
It's my time.

The race was hard, but I won.
It's my time.

All is peace and there is no fright.
It's my time.

I am ready for my heavenly flight.
It's my time!

In memory of my precious aunt Jackie

Isaiah 40:28–31 (New International Version)

²⁸Do you not know? Have you not heard? The LORD is the everlasting God, the Creator of the ends of the earth. He will not grow tired or weary, and his understanding no one can fathom. ²⁹He gives strength to the weary and increases the power of the weak. ³⁰Even youths grow tired and weary, and young men stumble and fall; ³¹but those who hope in the LORD will renew their strength. They will soar on wings like eagles; they will run and not grow weary, they will walk and not be faint.

My Aunt Jackie loved the above passage of scripture. She was always encouraged by the Word of God. How does this passage speak to you or your current situation?

_____

_____

_____

_____

_____

_____

_____

_____

_____

_____

_____

_____

_____

Thank You, Lord, for giving me time!

You can't go wrong
by doing right!

Proverbs 4:11 (New American Standard Bible)

[11]I have directed you in the way of wisdom;
I have led you in upright paths.

Just do the right thing. Sometimes, you may not have a clear picture of what that is. Well, seek the answer you need from our sweet Lord. What a comfort to know He will never mislead you. Finish this prayer: Lord, please lead and direct my paths. I need you to show me ...

_____

_____

_____

_____

_____

_____

_____

_____

_____

_____

_____

_____

_____

_____

_____

_____

Thank You, Lord, for leading me!

Where I belong!

Sitting at Your feet,
oh Lord, is where I long to be,
listening for your heart,
which surely beats for me.

Your hand so soft and tender
but strong enough to carry me.
Your eyes watch over me;
I want to be all that You see.

Help me to have Your ways, oh Lord,
and make me real from the start.
Give me Your love and Your perfect heart.

Psalm 55:22 (Contemporary English Version)

Our LORD, we belong to You. We tell You what worries us,
and You won't let us fall.

You belong to God. Others may have rejected you, but God will never fail you.
Share a time when you felt betrayed; how did God encourage you along?

_____

_____

_____

_____

_____

_____

_____

_____

_____

_____

_____

_____

_____

_____

_____

_____

_____

_____

Thank You, Lord, for holding me close!

Nanny Says ...

Silence is golden

Proverbs 17:28 (New Living Translation)

Even fools are thought wise when they keep silent;
with their mouths shut, they seem intelligent.

Shhhhh …

_____

_____

_____

_____

_____

_____

_____

_____

_____

_____

_____

_____

_____

Thank You, Lord, for silence!

Every Day

Help me, Lord, to look to You
in everything I say and do.

Always knowing it'll be all right,
If I don't use my worldly sight.

Learning to trust and obey
You to handle any problems
that come my way.

Walking in what I believe
and not in what I see.

Just to do Your will, I pray,
helps me live for You every day.

Lamentations 3:23 (New Living Translation)

Great is his faithfulness; His mercies begin afresh each morning.

You must focus on the Father! He will meet your daily needs. Many times, you will have to walk by faith and not by sight. Are you walking today with your eyes on Jesus or on the junk of this world?

_____

_____

_____

_____

_____

_____

_____

_____

_____

_____

_____

_____

_____

_____

_____

Thank You, Lord, for focus!

*P*eace is a Priceless

TREASURE

Philippians 4:6–7 (New Living Translation)

[6]Don't worry about anything; instead, pray about everything.
Tell God what you need, and thank Him for all He has
done. [7]Then you will experience God's peace, which exceeds
anything we can understand. His peace will guard your hearts
and minds as you live in Christ Jesus.

*Do not worry! That's what this sign is saying, along with the above Bible verse,
which is displayed in my bedroom. I can't tell you how many countless times I
have stood in front of it, reading those words and verses over and over…. What
worries you? The Lord says, "Do not worry!" He is Large and in Charge!*

_____

_____

_____

_____

_____

_____

_____

_____

_____

_____

_____

_____

_____

_____

Thank You, Lord, for peace!

I am PG

My life is PG rated,
that's the reason I was created.

So I carry my PG with me,
everywhere I must be.

I don't worry about my PG;
it's just a part of me.

It's down in my heart
and up in my head.

It the first thing I think of,
and the last when I hit the bed.

My PG is the biggest art of my story,
for you see, it's my Father's Pleasure and Glory.

So why don't you join with me,
and say "I am His PG!"

Psalm 104:31 (New Living Translation)

May the glory of the LORD continue forever!
The LORD takes pleasure in all He has made!

You were created to bring God pleasure and glory. In what ways do you bring God pleasure and glory? Yes, it can be by folding laundry! ☺

_____

_____

_____

_____

_____

_____

_____

_____

_____

_____

_____

_____

_____

_____

_____

_____

Thank You, Lord, for creating me!

When we see death, destruction, and the end,

GOD sees life, completion, as it just begins!

Philippians 1:21 (Contemporary English Version)

If I live, it will be for Christ, and if I die, I will gain even
more.

Do you look at death as the beginning or the end? In death, you will gain more
than this world has ever given you. Do you fear death? Why or why not?

_____

_____

_____

_____

_____

_____

_____

_____

_____

_____

_____

_____

_____

_____

_____

_____

_____

_____

Thank You, Lord, for even more!

My Journey to Jesus

Oh, my journey is so worry-free
because my Lord walks ahead of me.

Removing some obstacles along the way,
but also allowing a few to stay.

For these obstacles teach me something, Lord:
to lean on You a little bit more.

When You send joyful times,
that's when our heart beats close in rhyme.

Lord, as I daily walk Your journey's way,
help me learn from You every day.

I travel my journey to Jesus each day;
help me, Lord, to follow Your way.

Luke 13:33 (New King James Version)

Nevertheless, I must journey today, tomorrow,
and the *day* following.

Life is a daily journey. You are traveling somewhere. You are either walking toward Jesus or away from Him. In which direction are you traveling today?

_____

_____

_____

_____

_____

_____

_____

_____

_____

_____

_____

_____

_____

_____

_____

_____

_____

_____

Thank You, Lord, for direction!

Your weight is only a number;

it doesn't measure who you are in Christ!

Deuteronomy 25:15 (New King James Version)

You shall have a perfect and just weight, a perfect and just measure, that your days may be lengthened in the land the LORD your God is giving you.

Do you struggle with the scales? Try this simple prayer: "Less of me, more of You, Lord!" God loves you for who you are! Hallelujah—you have a perfect weight!

_____

_____

_____

_____

_____

_____

_____

_____

_____

_____

_____

_____

_____

_____

_____

_____

_____

_____

_____

Thank You, Lord, for my measurements!

Childhood Games

Faith as a child
is what You ask of me.
Lord, I don't have to
see to believe.

Sometimes fear comes to play
where my friend faith should stay.

Lord, as a little girl
in this big, dark world,
I get asked to play
with fear and doubt.

A good game of "Tag! You're it!"
But then I realize who is in control.

And as I Hopscotch my way to heaven's door,
my faith grows stronger all the more.

Ring Around the Rosy is fun all the while;
Lord, I just want to make You smile.

Life can be like a childhood game;
may I hop, skip, and jump in Jesus's name!

Matthew 19:14 (New Living Translation)

But Jesus said, "Let the children come to me. Don't stop them!
For the Kingdom of heaven belongs to those who are like
these children."

Do you remember the sweetness of your childhood? Share a fun childhood
memory. Go and enjoy some "playtime" with Jesus today.

_____

_____

_____

_____

_____

_____

_____

_____

_____

_____

_____

_____

_____

_____

_____

_____

Thank You, Lord, for laughter!

Get Right or Get Left!

JESUS is coming soon!

1 Corinthians 1:8 (New Living Translation)

He will keep you strong to the end so that you will be free
from all blame on the day when our Lord Jesus Christ returns.

*Praise the LORD! He is returning for His children. Are you ready? Write a
prayer to our sweet Lord in preparation for His return. "Ain't no high like the
Most High!"*

_____

_____

_____

_____

_____

_____

_____

_____

_____

_____

_____

_____

_____

_____

_____

_____

Thank You, Lord, for making me right!

Enduring It All

by Ansley Pealock Green

As innocent as a baby held by its mother.
Put on Earth to capture hearts.
Did the unexplainable.
Let the blind see.
Let the deaf hear.
Let the lame walk.
Nothing was impossible.
Yet all was humble.

It was destined.
Simple prayers were shared.
The time has come.
Do not stop what had to happen.

Taken over by betrayal.
Looked at as a liar, a victim of crime.
A life of pureness.
Corrupted by the world.
Life had been lived for this
appointment with death.

Took the stripes.
Hanging with compassion.
The sounds of harsh words.
Feeling the blood run down the brow.
Calling "Father."

Holding on till there was no more.
Looked into the clouds and saw relief.
It was silent, with the whispers of wind.
Knowing that the will was done.
The head was hung with ease.

The white robe was stained.
Blood had shattered like a window pane.
Yet not a bone broken.
Still so gentle and loving.
A figure hanging on a cross.
The rocks were crying out.
Horror met with love.
Love conquered.

No longer will you suffer.
Forget about your fears.
Life was breathed again.
The sun rose.
Alive with harmony.
Angels sang from above.
Miracles sprouted.
Forgiveness is why.
Walking and ministering.
Now watching from above.

Knowing that He lived to die.
Knowing He would give his life.
Knowing He would suffer with pain.
Knowing if He gave up he would lose us.
Keeping His arms stretched out wide on the cross.
The most innocent child was He.

Thank You, Lord, for enduring it all!

Shine On, Sista!

In a world so dark and dim,
I must shine for Him!
I can't hide it. Oh,
I'll never deny it!

When others look around to see,
can they tell who lives inside me?

Is it at the grocery store putting up my cart?
Or hanging up clothes, trying to do my part?

If I'm in aisle five and then decide
the bread from aisle two just won't do,
just leave it in aisle three.
Someone will come by and move it back for me.

Shine On, Sista!

Oh, we've all done it, no need to shun it.
Living like no one will see.

Oh, but wait—didn't He say that
He goes with me throughout my day?
Helping, watching, and leading the way!

Lord, You are here all the time,
Help me, please, to *shine*!

Shine On, Sista!

Matthew 5:16 (New International Version)

In the same way, let your light shine before men, that they may see your good deeds and praise your Father in heaven.

Your little deeds mean so much to God. If you're faithful with little, He'll give you much. What have you been doing that seems small? Do you see big things being produced from your faithfulness? Shine On, Sista! SOS!

_____

_____

_____

_____

_____

_____

_____

_____

_____

_____

_____

_____

_____

_____

_____

Thank You, Lord, for shining through me!

Notes

Notes

Notes

Notes

Notes

Notes

Notes

Notes

Notes

Notes

Notes

Notes

Notes

Notes

Notes

Notes

Notes

Notes

Notes

Notes

Notes

Notes

Notes

_____

_____

_____

_____

_____

_____

_____

_____

_____

_____

_____

_____

_____

_____

_____

_____

_____

_____

_____

_____

_____

_____

_____

_____

_____

Notes

Notes

Notes

Notes

Notes

About the Author

Staci Pealock lives in the mountains of Northeast Georgia. She and her husband, Todd, have been married for twenty-four years and have two grown children, Ansley, twenty-one, and Andrew, nineteen. Staci has served in various areas of ministry for more than twenty-six years and just recently obtained her exhorter's license through the Church of God. Currently, she coordinates the women's Bible studies at her church, where more than one hundred women attend on a weekly basis. Staci is the founder of the nonprofit organization Love And Ministry Between Sistas (LAMBS). She is the coordinator and speaker of a weekend women's conference called Divine Design—The House that God Built. Staci is known for her quick wit and one liners she likes to call her "Stacisms"—Lovin' Life and Lovin' the Lord! Staci is available to speak at women's events; you may contact her at stacip@hemc.net

LaVergne, TN USA
27 December 2010

210152LV00004B/34/P